I0820568

Romeo and Juliet

Lightbox Literature Studies

Piper Whelan

Go to
www.openlightbox.com
and enter this book's
unique code.

ACCESS CODE

LBV45824

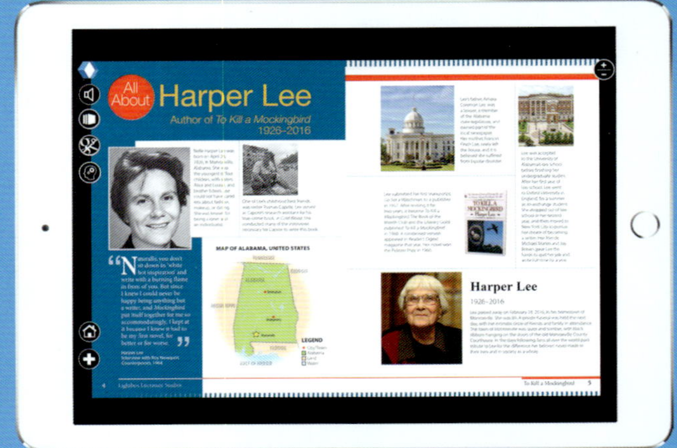

Lightbox is an all-inclusive digital solution for the teaching and learning of curriculum topics in an original, groundbreaking way. Lightbox is based on National Curriculum Standards.

STANDARD FEATURES OF LIGHTBOX

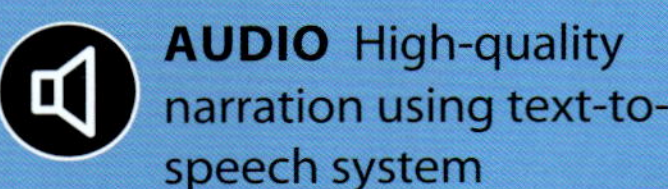

AUDIO High-quality narration using text-to-speech system

VIDEOS Embedded high-definition video clips

ACTIVITIES Printable PDFs that can be emailed and graded

WEBLINKS Curated links to external, child-safe resources

SLIDESHOWS Pictorial overviews of key concepts

TRANSPARENCIES Step-by-step layering of maps, diagrams, charts, and timelines

INTERACTIVE MAPS Interactive maps and aerial satellite imagery

QUIZZES Ten multiple choice questions that are automatically graded and emailed for teacher assessment

KEY WORDS Matching key concepts to their definitions

MORE Extra information and details on the subject

FIRST HAND Letters, diaries, and other primary sources

DOCS Speeches, newspaper articles, and other historical documents

Copyright © 2018 Smartbook Media Inc. All rights reserved.

Contents

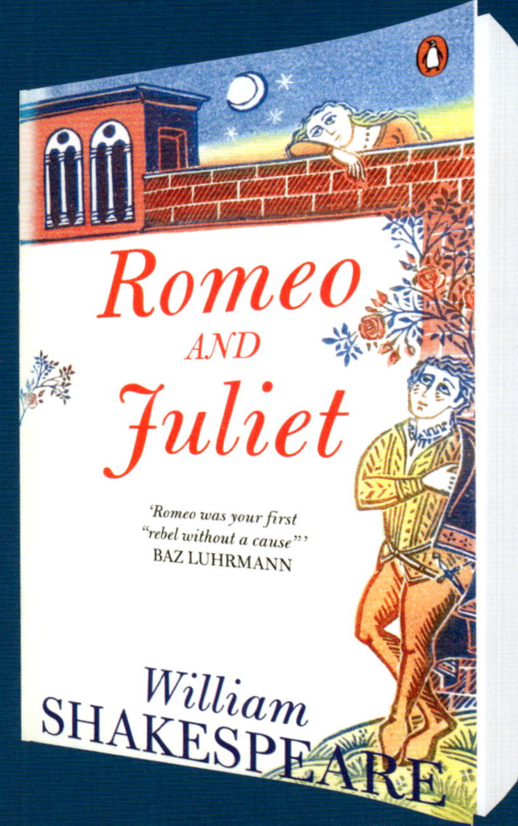
Romeo
AND
Juliet
'Romeo was your first "rebel without a cause"'
BAZ LUHRMANN
William
SHAKESPEARE

EXTENSION ACTIVITY

Conducting an Interview

Students will conduct an interview with a community member about a time period in their community's history, and submit an audio recording and transcript of the interview. An exemplary interview will meet the following criteria.

- Clearly defines the purpose of the interview
- Conducts thorough background research to inform the focus of the interview and the questions
- Drafts a complete list of thoughtful, in-depth, and varied questions prior to the interview
- Interviews a subject with relevant knowledge on the topic and time period in question
- Asks questions in a logical order, building upon each other
- Treats the interview subject in a polite, respectful, and professional manner
- Does not interrupt or rush the interview subject
- Shows interest and enthusiasm in responses and follow-up questions
- Chooses follow-up questions that demonstrate active listening
- Asks for clarification and further details when necessary
- Asks questions about personal experiences related to the topic
- Asks questions regarding factual information and the interview subject's opinion on the topic
- Asks creative questions that reflect fresh insights on the topic
- Records the full interview in a quiet environment
- Organizes and edits the interview transcript to be clear and factual

William Shakespeare

Author of *Romeo and Juliet*

1564–1616

William Shakespeare was baptized on April 26, 1564, in Stratford-upon-Avon, England. His father, John Shakespeare, was a leatherworker and well-known businessman, and held several positions in local government. His mother, Mary Arden, came from a prominent local family of higher social standing.

It is likely that Shakespeare attended a local grammar school. As was the custom of the time, his education would have had a major focus on Latin. It is believed that Shakespeare attended school until he was about 15, and he did not go on to study at a university afterward.

> **"Have more than thou showest,/Speak less than thou knowest,/Lend less than thou owest,/Ride more than thou goest,/Learn more than thou trowest,/Set less than thou throwest..."**
>
> William Shakespeare, *King Lear*, Act 1, Scene 4, Circa 1605

MAP OF THE UNITED KINGDOM

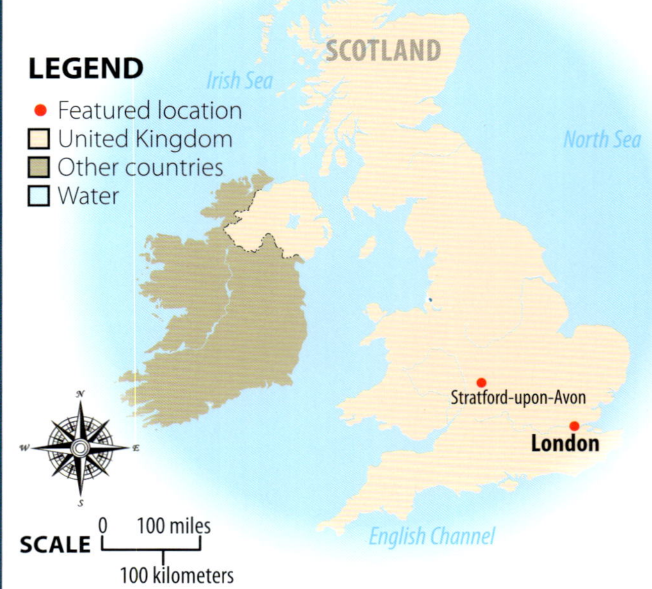

TEACHER NOTES

Shakespeare was 18 in 1582 when he married Anne Hathaway, who was 26. They had two daughters, Susanna and Judith, and one son, Hamnet. Hamnet died in 1596, when he was 11 years old. Shakespeare's family lived in Stratford while he worked in London, pursuing a career in theater.

After his children were born, there were a number of years where experts are unsure of what Shakespeare was doing. There are many stories about how he may have earned a living, but nothing is certain until his name shows up in records related to London's theaters. The first mention of Shakespeare as an actor and playwright came in 1592, and around 1594, he became a key member of the Lord Chamberlain's Men theater company. He also published his first poems around this time.

Shakespeare was a playwright, an actor, and later a business partner in the Lord Chamberlain's Men for more than 20 years. He became increasingly famous around London for his plays. The company, which became known as the King's Men in 1603, performed Shakespeare's works, and he found a full-time career as a playwright. His financial success in theater is evident, as he bought the second-largest house in Stratford in 1597. In total, he wrote 38 plays and more than 150 poems.

Shakespeare died on April 23, 1616, at the age of 52. His cause of death is unknown, and his gravestone in the churchyard in Stratford does not have his name inscribed upon it. Four lines were inscribed on it instead, which some believe he may have composed. They read, "Good friend, for Jesus' sake forbear/To dig the dust enclosed here./Blest be the man that spares these stones./And curst be he that move my bones."

Google Maps

Shakespeare's Birthplace, Stratford-upon-Avon, Warwickshire, England

Explore Shakespeare's hometown using the street view of his birthplace, now a heritage site, and the surrounding streets of Stratford-upon-Avon.

First Hand

Douglas Booth, Hailee Steinfeld & Director Carlo Carlei Interview, Romeo & Juliet

Examine this interview with the director and stars of the 2013 film, *Romeo & Juliet*.

1. What types of questions does the interviewer ask? What topics does he focus on? Why would he focus on these specific areas?
2. How has the classic story been reimagined in this adaptation? How were the characters adapted for the screen?
3. Why are people so fascinated with the concept of tragedy in love? Why does Shakespeare's story remain as timeless, entertaining, and relatable today as when it was first performed on stage?

EXTENSION ACTIVITY

Researching for a Writing Assignment

Students will complete a thorough research process to prepare for a writing assignment, and organize their research in a logical manner that supports their writing. An exemplary research process will meet the following criteria.

- Creates a goal for the research, based on the topic and working thesis
- Creates specific, thoughtful, and inventive research questions that are relevant to the topic of the writing assignment
- Produces a list of categories, key words, and related ideas to effectively assist in researching
- Uses high-quality sources that pertain to the topic and come in a variety of formats, such as books, journals, primary sources, websites, and databases
- Determines accuracy of all sources
- Uses sources that provide balanced research and various perspectives on the topic in question
- Takes notes to highlight the key facts and ideas in order to answer all research questions
- Extracts relevant, detailed information from the sources during the note-taking process
- Organizes the research notes in a clear and concise manner
- Organizes the research notes logically and in a way that sets up the information and ideas for analysis and the writing process
- Analyzes the information and produces ideas and points to support the working thesis
- Uses an effective and suitable format to present all research
- Properly cites all sources used

Setting of the Play

Shakespeare set *Romeo and Juliet* in Verona, Italy. This city is located in the province of Verona, which is in the Veneto region of northern Italy, near the Lessini Mountains. Shakespeare's tragic play made Verona famous, and tourists from all over the world visit the city each year. A city already filled with centuries of history, Verona's identity has become forever linked to *Romeo and Juliet*.

Snapshot

Verona, Italy

The city of Verona was **founded** in the **first century** BC.

Verona became a **UNESCO World Heritage Site** in **2000**.

UNESCO

Verona is the **fourth most-visited** city in Italy.

Shakespeare's Verona

"Two households, both alike in dignity,
In fair Verona, where we lay our scene,
From ancient grudge break to new mutiny,
Where civil blood makes civil hands unclean.
From forth the fatal loins of these two foes
A pair of star-crossed lovers take their life,
Whose misadventured piteous overthrows;
Doth with their death bury their parents' strife."

Chorus, Prologue

Arguably Verona's most popular tourist destination, the building known as Juliet's House was built in the thirteenth century, and once belonged to the Del Capello, or Cappelletti, family. Today, visitors tour the house and stand on its balcony, much like the one in the play's well-known balcony scene. Visitors also leave messages addressed to Juliet on the courtyard wall under the balcony in hopes of finding true love. Many fans of the play also write letters to Juliet for that same purpose, which are replied to by a group of volunteers called the Juliet Club.

Verona is also notable for its many well-preserved historical sites, dating back to the **Renaissance** period, and some even back to Roman rule. One such Roman ruin is Verona's amphitheater, which is the third-largest amphitheater from the time of the Roman Empire. It was built in the first century AD, and today, still has most of its original stone. The amphitheater, which was once the venue for battles between Roman gladiators, now hosts plays and the city's summer opera festival.

TEACHER NOTES

Video

The Setting of Romeo and Juliet: City of Verona
Find out more about Verona by watching this video.

1. Why do many buildings in Verona have crown-shaped features? What do these features indicate? How are they connected to *Romeo and Juliet*?
2. Why was Verona chosen as the setting for this tragic love story? How do you think the play would be different if it were set in another city? Give reasons for your answer.

Weblink

Juliet Club
Learn more about the Juliet Club by visiting this website.

1. Why is Verona known as the "town of love"?
2. How might writing a letter to Juliet help readers feel more connected to the play?
3. Do you think the practice of hand writing letters is outdated or is there value in keeping this epistolary tradition alive? Explain your position.

EXTENSION ACTIVITY

Analyzing a Newspaper Article

Students will assess a newspaper article and write an analysis. An exemplary analysis will meet the following criteria.

- Identifies the topic of the article
- Identifies the main points and opinions presented in the article
- Identifies the writer of the article
- Presents information about the writer and infers how his or her life may have shaped this opinion
- Assesses the writer's reliability
- Analyzes how the writer makes his or her argument
- Uses evidence from the article to show how the writer supports his or her argument
- Analyzes the writer's use of literary devices to enhance the article
- Differentiates between the facts and opinions presented in the article
- Identifies when and where the article was published, and determines its intended audience
- Identifies and understands the goals of the article
- Assesses the effectiveness of the format (a newspaper opinion article) in presenting the writer's argument
- Connects the article to the societal and historical context in which it was written
- Infers what is not said about this topic in the article
- Identifies what information is unintentionally implied in the article
- Infers what other opinions may be presented about this topic and who may be most likely to express them
- Uses a number of other resources to analyze the context of the article

Time Period of the Play

Shakespeare wrote *Romeo and Juliet* in the early years of his career as a playwright, likely during the early or mid-1590s. The play itself is set in an earlier century, coinciding with the Renaissance era. Beginning in Italy, this period had a great impact on literature in Shakespeare's time. The following excerpt from *Romeo and Juliet*, taken together, creates a sonnet, one of the forms of poetry that came to England from the Italian Renaissance.

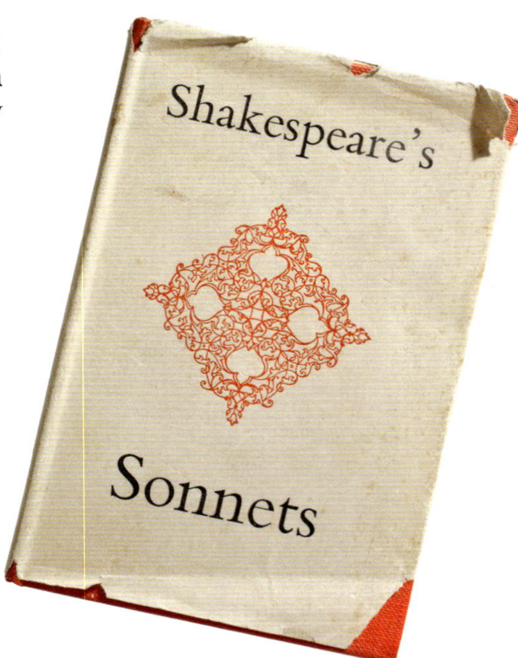

The Use of Sonnets

Romeo: "If I profane with my unworthiest hand
This holy shrine, the gentle sin is this:
My lips, two blushing pilgrims, ready stand
To smooth that rough touch with a tender kiss."
Juliet: "Good pilgrim, you do wrong your hand too much,
Which mannerly devotion shows in this,
For saints have hands that pilgrims' hands do touch,
And palm to palm is holy palmers' kiss."
Romeo: "Have not saints lips, and holy palmers too?"
Juliet: "Ay, pilgrim, lips that they must use in prayer."
Romeo: "O, then, dear saint, lest lips do what
hands do:
They pray, grant thou, lest faith turn to despair."
Juliet: "Saints do not move, though grant for prayers' sake."
Romeo: "Then move not, while my prayer's effect I take."

Romeo and Juliet, Act 1, Scene 4

The Renaissance was a time of artistic and scientific development that greatly shaped Italian culture in the fourteenth and fifteenth centuries, the effects of which later spread throughout Europe. The name *Renaissance* means "rebirth," and reflects the cultural explosion that created a new era after the Middle Ages. During the Italian Renaissance, there was a renewal of popularity in classical Greek and Roman art, and there were numerous advances in art, literature, architecture, and science.

Despite a lack of evidence to support this claim, some believe that Shakespeare's lost years in the 1580s were spent in Italy, as his forms of poetry and use of the country as a setting in a number of his plays suggests his interest. Regardless, English writers in the sixteenth century became interested in Italian literature written during the Renaissance, which became soon available in England. Italian literature inspired many English poets, including Shakespeare, and the forms of poetry that were most popular in the Elizabethan Age came from Italian works.

Shakespeare's writing was influenced by the Italian poet Francesco Petrarca, also known as Petrarch. Writing during the fourteenth century, Petrarch developed the sonnet, and English writers drew inspiration primarily from his work in this form of poetry. Shakespeare, who would go on to become celebrated for his own sonnets, references Petrarch's sonnets written for his love, Laura, in Act 2, Scene 3 of *Romeo and Juliet*. This allusion highlights Romeo's lovestruck state.

TEACHER NOTES

Video

Shakespeare's Sonnets: Crash Course Literature 304

Discover more about sonnets and their history by watching this video.

1. Why did Shakespeare think poetry was important? Do you agree with his assertion? Why or why not?
2. How did the time period that Shakespeare's sonnets were written in affect his use of the form? Do you think he would still write poetry if he were alive today or would another form of expression be more appropriate? Give reasons for your answer.

Weblink

Was Shakespeare a teacher? Villagers claim the Bard spent his 'lost years' working as a humble schoolmaster

Review the *Daily Mail* article by Amanda Williams, published on April 8, 2013, about Shakespeare's lost years.

1. What evidence supports the theory that Shakespeare spent three years as a schoolmaster in Titchfield, Hampshire? Do you support this theory? Why or why not? Explain your position.
2. What stance, if any, does the author take?

EXTENSION ACTIVITY

Writing a Short Story

Students will choose an excerpt from the play and use it as their inspiration in writing a short story. An exemplary short story will meet the following criteria.

- Engages the reader from the opening line
- Establishes a clear, consistent point of view
- Introduces a narrator and a setting
- Develops an engaging conflict at the heart of the narrative to build tension and keep the reader interested
- Develops characters and events through purposeful and well-crafted literary devices
- Creates a logical progression of events in the narrative that build upon each other using various techniques
- Explores ideas, concepts, and writing styles with creativity and originality
- Demonstrates a high level of skill in using appropriate narrative techniques to tell the story
- Concludes the narrative in a thoughtful, effective manner appropriate to the narrative
- Uses varied, purposeful diction and syntax to affect style and serve the narrative
- Writes with clarity, imagination, and a unique, personal voice
- Does not use stereotypes or clichés
- Uses effective, believable dialogue
- Uses correct spelling, grammar, and punctuation

Conflict in the Play

In literature, conflict is a struggle between two or more opposing forces, creating a tension that must be resolved. This is the main challenge that the protagonist faces throughout the story. This struggle is often between the protagonist and antagonist, but there are other types of conflict found in literature. Conflict is a vital element in any piece of literature. Without it, there is no story.

The Four Major Types of Conflict in Literature

CHARACTER vs. CHARACTER

In this type of conflict, the protagonist struggles with an opposing character, usually the antagonist. This is common in fiction, and generally features the fight between good and evil. However, not all character versus character conflicts are between protagonist and antagonist. For example, in *The Outsiders*, Ponyboy Curtis often clashes with his brother Darry.

CHARACTER vs. SELF

The protagonist fights an inner battle in a character versus self conflict. The battle is often about a major decision, and the internal issue then affects his or her actions and motivation. In *Pride and Prejudice*, Elizabeth Bennet realizes she has misjudged the character of two young men, and struggles with the decisions she made based upon these judgments.

CHARACTER vs. SOCIETY

In character versus **society** conflict, the protagonist is opposed to the principles or actions of his or her community, or of society as a whole. This conflict is based upon the protagonist's beliefs or **morals**. This kind of conflict appears in *Of Mice and Men*, as George Milton and Lennie Small travel to find work, and try to survive during the Great Depression in a society that is not kind to those who are different.

CHARACTER vs. NATURE

The protagonist faces an obstacle in nature in character versus nature conflict. The obstacle may be an entire landscape, or a symbolic representation of nature, such as an animal or natural disaster. In *Lord of the Flies*, a group of marooned schoolboys fight to stay alive on an island, which leads to other kinds of conflict.

Types of Conflict in *Romeo and Juliet*

The two main types of conflict in *Romeo and Juliet* are character versus character and character versus self. Each of these conflicts plays a major role in the story.

Character versus Character

Romeo: Alive, in triumph! and
Mercutio slain!
Away to heaven, respective lenity,
And fire and fury be my conduct now!
Now, Tybalt, take the 'villain' back again,
That late thou gav'st me, for Mercutio's soul
Is but a little way above our heads,
Staying for thine to keep him company:
Either thou or I, or both, must go with him.
Tybalt: Thou, wretched boy, that didst
consort him here,
Shalt with him hence.
Romeo: This shall determine that.

Romeo and Tybalt, Act 3, Scene 1

Character versus Self

"My only love sprung from my only hate!
Too early seen unknown, and known
too late!
Prodigious birth of love it is to me,
That I must love a loathed enemy."

Juliet, Act 1, Scene 4

TEACHER NOTES

More

The Types of Conflict in *Romeo and Juliet*

Analyze the excerpts from the play revealing the types of conflict as they appear in *Romeo and Juliet*.

1. How do these excerpts of conflict reveal the play's theme? How do they reveal character? Explain and defend your ideas.
2. Write an analysis of Shakespeare's development of conflict between the Montagues and the Capulets. What deeper truths may be suggested about these characters as a result of their conflict?

Weblink

Conflict

Review the lesson about conflict in *Romeo and Juliet*.

1. What are the goals of this lesson? How is it structured to accomplish these goals? Is it successful in doing so? What improvements, if any, would you suggest to make it more effective?
2. Compare and contrast the conflicts between the two warring families, Juliet's inner conflict, and the conflict between Tybalt and Romeo. How are they similar? In what ways are they different? How does Shakespeare demonstrate each type of conflict? Give specific examples from the text to support your answer.

EXTENSION ACTIVITY

Holding a Classroom Debate

Students will form groups and prepare arguments for a debate on a controversial issue. Exemplary performance in a debate will meet the following criteria.

- Demonstrates in-depth understanding of the topic and related information
- Presents strong, logical, and convincing arguments
- Communicates in a clear and confident manner
- Maintains eye contact
- Uses clear vocal tone and a reasonable rate of vocal delivery
- Uses respectful and appropriate language and body language
- Delivers arguments, evidence, and counter-evidence in an engaging and persuasive manner
- Supports each major point of an argument with several relevant and detailed facts and examples
- Connects all arguments to the overall topic in a clear, concise, and organized manner
- Presents the arguments and supporting evidence in a clear, logical manner
- Presents clear, thorough, and accurate information throughout the debate
- Addresses all of the opposing team's arguments with counter-arguments
- Identifies any weakness in the opposing team's arguments
- Constructs strong and relevant counter-arguments using accurate information
- Presents strong and persuasive arguments throughout the debate
- Summarizes the arguments in the closing statement

Introducing the Characters

Writers use direct and indirect methods to reveal their characters. Successful writers tend to rely on indirect methods of character development. It is more effective to learn about characters by watching them in action rather than being told what they are like. When writers comment on their characters' personalities, they often do so through the eyes of other characters who see things from their own limited **perspectives**. In *Romeo and Juliet*, the only character description is provided through dialogue, as there is no formal narrator.

Major Characters in *Romeo and Juliet*

Most stories have a protagonist and antagonist. The protagonist is the central character who must resolve a conflict over the course of the story, and often develops as a character as a result of facing this conflict. Romeo and Juliet are the protagonists of the play. Together, they face conflict in the form of their warring families, and individually, they deal with internal conflicts related to love, family, and **loyalty**. Both characters also face conflict from another character. Romeo is antagonized by Tybalt, and Juliet clashes with her father over the issue of marriage.

The antagonist is the character or force who stands in opposition to the protagonist. In some cases, he or she creates or represents the conflict that the protagonist has to overcome. Tybalt is the primary antagonist in *Romeo and Juliet*. His anger toward the Montagues furthers the **feud** between the two families, and it is his actions that lead, in part, to the downfall of both Romeo and Juliet.

There are many characters who assist in moving the plot forward. Dynamic characters, such as the elder Montagues and Capulets, change throughout the story, usually after facing conflict. A static character does not undergo changes. A flat character, such as the Nurse, has only one distinguishing personality trait. A rounded character, such as Mercutio, has a more complex personality.

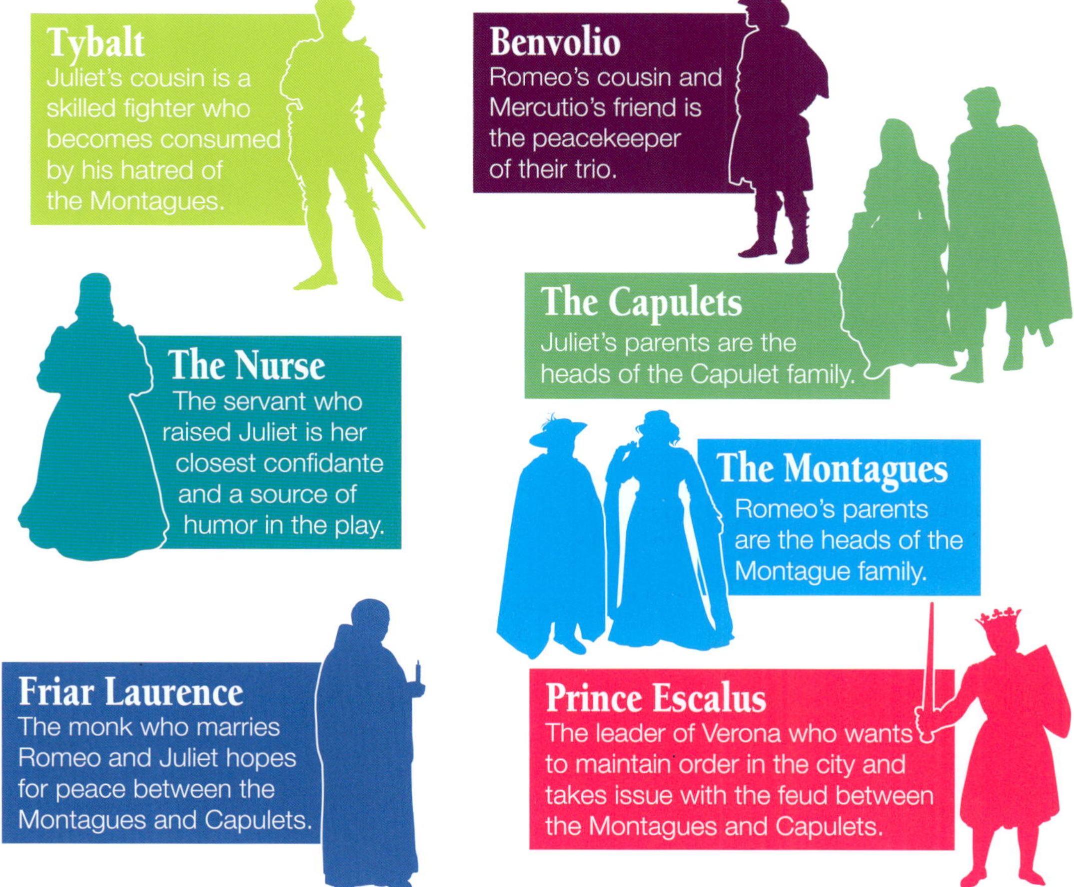

TEACHER NOTES

Weblink

Character Analysis Friar Laurence

Review a character analysis of Friar Laurence and debate his role in *Romeo and Juliet*.

1. Is Friar Laurence trustworthy? Why or why not?
2. Do you think Friar Laurence is to blame for the deaths of Romeo and Juliet? Give textual evidence to support your claim.

More

Character Development in *Romeo and Juliet*

Analyze the characters in *Romeo and Juliet* using the descriptions on the character map and excerpts from each character. Then, choose a character and answer the following questions.

1. Which of the writer's techniques are most effective at revealing this character's traits? Why?
2. In what ways is the characterization of this character ineffective? What could be done to improve this character's function in the play? Defend your ideas with evidence.

EXTENSION ACTIVITY

Creating a Literary Device Analysis Booklet

Students will analyze the author's use of a literary device in the play, and create a booklet to present this analysis. An exemplary literary device analysis booklet will meet the following criteria.

- Defines the chosen literary device accurately and in detail
- Places the definition of the literary device at the beginning of the booklet
- Provides strong, specific examples of how this literary device is used in the play
- Describes examples in detail, with quotations properly integrated
- Includes thorough analysis of the use, purpose, and effectiveness of each example of how the chosen literary device is used in the play
- Arranges all pages logically
- Examples are organized chronologically
- Provides no more than one example and its analysis per page
- Creates a neat, well-organized, and attractive booklet
- Booklet is colorful and displays the student's creativity
- Uses illustrations to represent the chosen literary device and the examples of how it is used in the play

The Art of Storytelling

Storytelling is a way to entertain, engage with others, teach, or communicate perspectives on society. A narrative, or story, is a series of events that is often logically arranged. When writing his or her story, a writer structures the narrative in a particular way. The writer can also use different types of literary devices to create a distinct style and to convey the narrative's overall message. In order to tell his story effectively, Shakespeare structured his narrative within the framework of a script, created a plot, and used a number of literary devices in *Romeo and Juliet*.

Structure of a Narrative

Every narrative has a structure that writers keep in mind when creating a story. The most common narrative structure, known as dramatic structure, or Freytag's Pyramid, consists of five main components, all of which are used in *Romeo and Juliet*. This structure functions within the five-act framework used in Shakespeare's plays.

Freytag's Pyramid

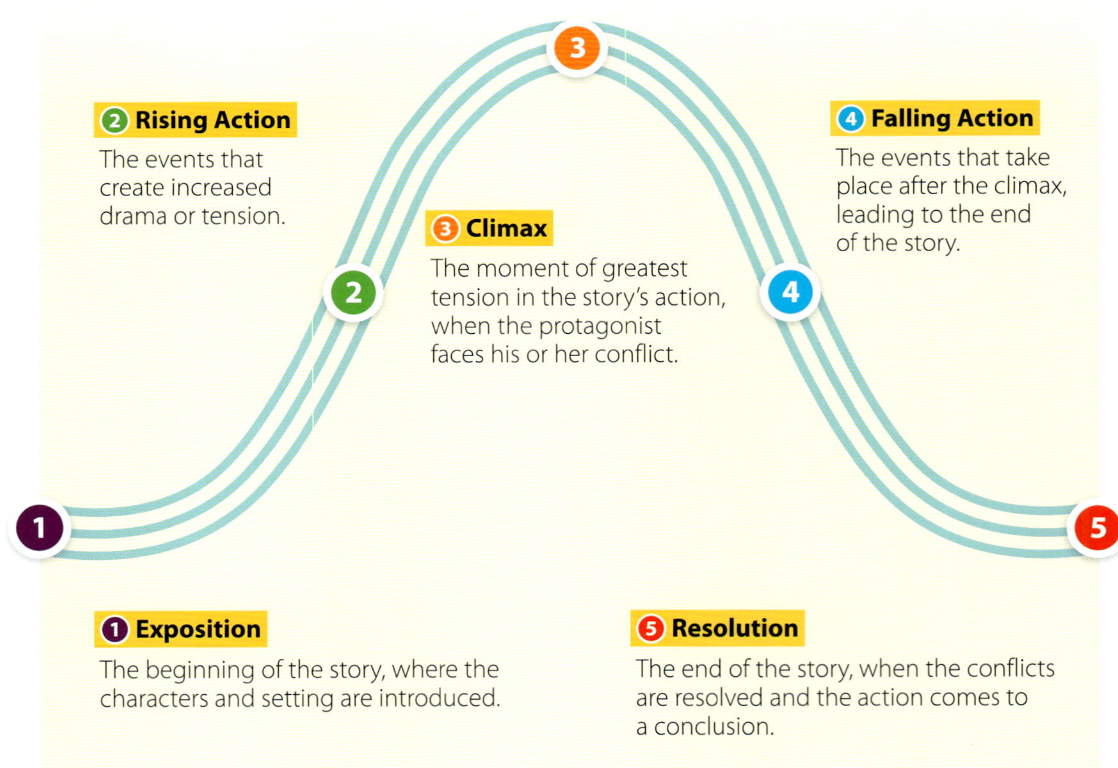

Plot

Every narrative needs to have a plot. Plot is the series of actions that propel the story forward. The plotline is the order in which events, or plot points, take place. These events build on each other and are organized in a logical manner. Each event causes the next event to happen, thus creating the narrative.

Plot Points in Act 1, Scene 4 of *Romeo and Juliet*

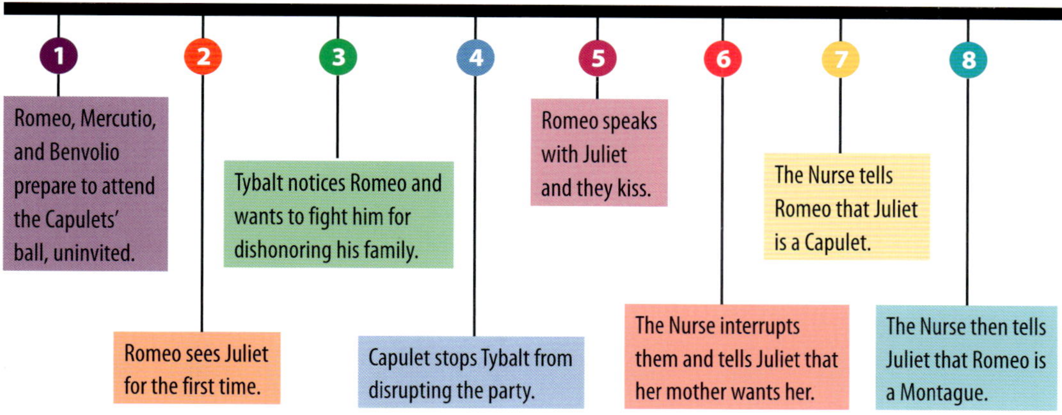

Literary Devices

A literary device is any particular feature of a work of literature that can be identified, studied, and analyzed. There are two types of literary devices. These are literary elements and literary techniques.

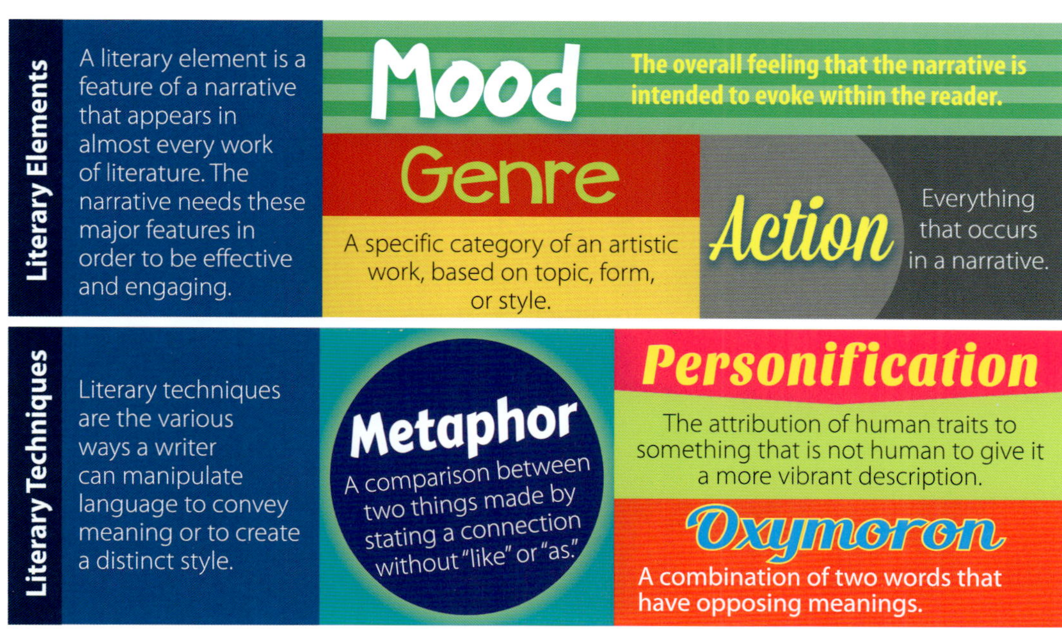

TEACHER NOTES

Weblink

Literary Devices

Find out more about literary elements and literary techniques.

1. What is the difference between a literary element and a literary technique? Explain in your own words, using examples from *Romeo and Juliet*.
2. What are some examples of popular literary devices? How do they contribute to a reader's overall experience, understanding, and enjoyment of a literary work?

More

Examples of Literary Techniques from the Play

Analyze the author's use of literary techniques and how they contribute to the narrative of *Romeo and Juliet*.

1. Choose one literary technique used in the play. In what particular way did the author use this literary technique? How effective was its usage?
2. What arguments can be made for the use of your chosen literary technique in a text? If this technique were overused or underutilized, what effect might it have on an author's work?

Theme in the Play

The theme of a story is the underlying idea or position about the topic of the overall work. It is often a general, **universal** statement about life. Sometimes, the theme is clearly stated, and other times it is subtly suggested.

A theme is different from the topic of a literary work. While a topic is the subject of a work, a theme makes a statement about the topic in question. Theme can be expressed through the events that take place in the story, the ideas repeated along the way, and the lessons the characters learn. The theme of a story is often open to **interpretation**. A reader may have to examine many different aspects of a work of literature in order to form an opinion about its themes.

Major Themes of *Romeo and Juliet*

Romeo and Juliet is one of Shakespeare's best-known plays, due to its romantic and tragic narrative. Audiences and readers respond strongly to its story of forbidden love, clan feuds, and loyalty. The play presents this narrative through its major themes of love, **fate**, and the individual against society.

Love

"Oh, she doth teach the torches to burn bright!
It seems she hangs upon the cheek of night
Like a rich jewel in an Ethiope's ear,
Beauty too rich for use, for earth too dear.
So shows a snowy dove trooping with crows
As yonder lady o'er her fellows shows.
The measure done, I'll watch her place of stand,
And, touching hers, make blessèd my rude hand.
Did my heart love till now? Forswear it, sight!
For I ne'er saw true beauty till this night."

Romeo, Act 1, Scene 4

Fate

Balthasar: "Then she is well, and nothing can be ill:
Her body sleeps in Capel's monument,
And her immortal part with angels lives.
I saw her laid low in her kindred's vault,
And presently took post to tell it you.
O, pardon me for bringing these ill news,
Since you did leave it for my office, sir."
Romeo: "Is it even so? Then I deny you, stars!"

Balthasar and Romeo, Act 5, Scene 1

The Individual Against Society

"O Romeo, Romeo! wherefore art thou Romeo?
Deny thy father and refuse thy name;
Or, if thou wilt not, be but sworn my love,
And I'll no longer be a Capulet."

Juliet, Act 2, Scene 1

Secondary Themes

Secondary themes are those that are not heavily emphasized in the narrative. While it does not play as large a role as a major theme, a secondary theme adds another layer to the ideas presented by the story, allowing for a more complex narrative and deeper literary analysis. Examples of secondary themes explored in *Romeo and Juliet* include violence and **gender roles**.

TEACHER NOTES

Weblink

Fate
Find out more about fate in *Romeo and Juliet*.

1. What is fate? Do you believe that the fates of Romeo and Juliet were predetermined? Why or why not? Give textual evidence to support your opinion.
2. How do you think an Elizabethan audience would have interpreted the fate of the "star-crossed lovers"? Why?

More

Major and Secondary Themes
Analyze the author's development of themes over the course of the play.

1. Choose a secondary theme from this spread and analyze its appearances in the play. How does this theme first emerge? Which is the most poignant example of this theme in the play?
2. What particular commentary might the author be making about life as a result of this theme's presence in the text? Explain and defend your ideas.
3. Choose a major theme presented on pages 16–17. In what ways does your chosen secondary theme relate to this major theme? Does it deepen or detract from the major theme? How or in what way?

EXTENSION ACTIVITY

Creating a Symbolism Poster

Students will choose one of the other symbols listed on page 19 and analyze its role in the play. They will then create a poster to present their analysis. An exemplary symbolism poster will meet the following criteria.

- Presents a clear purpose that is conveyed throughout the poster
- Shows an understanding of the concept of symbolism and the role it has in the play
- Provides an in-depth analysis of what the symbol represents
- Discusses the role the symbol has in the play
- Clearly indicates where the symbol appears in the play
- Uses specific, detailed examples from the text to support the analysis
- Makes clear connections to the text
- Properly integrates all quotations
- Organizes the information in a logical, easy-to-read manner
- Includes high-quality graphics that relate to the symbol and effectively enhance understanding of the topic
- Features clear and concise writing
- Uses correct spelling, grammar, and punctuation
- Clearly labels items of importance
- Headings and subheadings are clear and easy to read
- Uses layout to creatively enhances the information
- Creates a poster that is attractive in terms of layout, design, and organization
- Shows a strong effort by the student

Symbolism in the Play

Symbolism is a literary technique writers use to help convey theme. A symbol is often a tangible object to which a writer lends deeper meaning. Other times, action or dialogue in the narrative can be symbolic of a specific idea or theme.

Symbolism helps to give the story's events, characters, and themes a universal feel. Sometimes, it sheds light on how the writer feels about specific concepts and ideas. When studying a work of literature, the reader can gain a deeper understanding of the story by identifying and analyzing the symbols used by the writer. If the reader has trouble identifying symbols in the novel, a good place to look first is the work's title.

Light and Darkness

"Sleep dwell upon thine eyes, peace in thy breast!
Would I were sleep and peace, so sweet to rest!
The grey-eyed morn smiles on the frowning night,
Check'ring the eastern clouds with streaks of light,
And darkness fleckled like a drunkard reels
From forth day's pathway, made by Titan's wheels."

Romeo, Act 2, Scene 1

Light and Darkness as Symbols

Rather than the traditional symbolism of light and dark representing good and evil, Shakespeare uses these symbols in a more complicated way in *Romeo and Juliet*, which is also connected to the symbolism of day and night. By using this imagery, he creates a contrast for the senses and shows alternatives to the lives the characters are used to. An example of this symbolism appears in the iconic balcony scene, when Romeo compares Juliet to the Sun. Later in the play, Juliet compares Romeo to the stars. Though they see each other as forms of brilliant light, representing their love for each other, the darkness of night is the safest place to meet, as daylight forces them to separate. However, to make the two characters appear as bright lights to each other, the darkness of night must be present to make the feeling stronger. Nighttime gives the couple privacy, and symbolizes the freedom to release the **inhibitions** of the daytime, as Romeo and Juliet act bolder when together at night than they do in daylight.

Where Do Light and Darkness Appear in the Play?

The balcony scene, from Romeo's perspective

The balcony scene, from Juliet's perspective

Before Romeo is exiled from Verona

Other Symbols in the Play

Poison

The poison used in the play brings about the deaths of the lead characters, and symbolizes how hate leads to violence and death. Friar Laurence notes that all things in nature can be used for both good and evil, suggesting that poison truly becomes deadly through human intervention. This is certainly the case for Juliet's sleeping potion, which should have set the couple free, but instead led to both of their deaths.

Queen Mab

Prior to sneaking into the Capulets' ball, Mercutio speaks at length about Queen Mab, a fairy who brings dreams in the night. This speech highlights that her dreams push the dreamers toward their favorite vices. Mercutio speaks vividly of nonsense here. This speech represents the power in dreams and desires, but argues that these desires are as silly as the idea of Queen Mab, yet also have the ability to corrupt people. This view of desire and love contrasts with the version of love presented by Romeo and Juliet.

TEACHER NOTES

More

Where Do Light and Darkness Appear in the Play?
Assess the author's use of symbolism in the play.

1. Choose a perspective from the chart and analyze what the symbols of light and darkness represents in relation to it. For which character are these symbols the most poignant in the play? For which character are the symbols least poignant? Argue your opinions with clear reasons.
2. How are these symbols used or reflected in the play's themes? Illustrate the ways in which the author's use of language deepens or weakens the meaning of light and darkness as symbols. Explain and defend your ideas.

Weblink

***Romeo and Juliet*: Queen Mab**
Examine the article about Queen Mab in *Romeo and Juliet*.

1. Shakespeare was the first person to reference Queen Mab in English literature. How did this affect her popularity among other authors? Why do you think this is the case?
2. What particular commentary might the author be making about life as a result of this theme's presence in the text? Explain and defend your ideas.

EXTENSION ACTIVITY

Analyzing a Video

Students will watch and assess a video related to a component of the play, and write an analysis of the video. An exemplary video analysis will meet the following criteria.

- Identifies the purpose of the video
- Identifies the intended audience of the video
- Describes how the content of the video is presented
- Summarizes the information and opinions presented in the video
- Analyzes the quality of the content presented in the video
- Assesses the effectiveness of the video
- Discusses the technical aspects of the video and whether or not these enhance the content
- Determines whether the images and graphics used in the video relate to the content
- Determines whether the video is easy to follow and understand
- Gives the analysis a clear and consistent purpose
- Organizes the analysis in a logical, effective manner
- Presents a strong, clear argument about the video
- Provides strong and accurate details to support the argument about the video
- Considers other perspectives on the purpose and effectiveness of the video
- Makes connections between the video and the play
- Properly integrates quotations from the video
- Cites all sources used in the analysis

The Use of Language

Shakespeare had a major impact on the English language, coining numerous phrases now used every day, and even creating his own words. Experts believe that Shakespeare invented more than 1,600 new words, using combinations of words and anglicizing words from other languages. Shakespeare's considerable skill with words is evident in *Romeo and Juliet*, as he uses one of the poetic forms he is best known for to tell a story full of wordplay and double meanings.

Iambic Pentameter

Poetry is spoken or written according to a pattern, which is usually rhythmic. The major units in poetry are the line and verse, and lines can be further broken down into poetic feet. A poetic foot is a combination of stressed and unstressed syllables, creating a unit of rhythm, or meter. Shakespeare wrote his plays in a poetic meter called iambic pentameter. This particular type of poetic meter gives his dialogue a distinct rhythm and sound when performed. This uses an iambic foot, in which an unstressed syllable is followed by a stressed syllable, and there are about five iambic feet in each line. The rhythm follows this sound pattern:

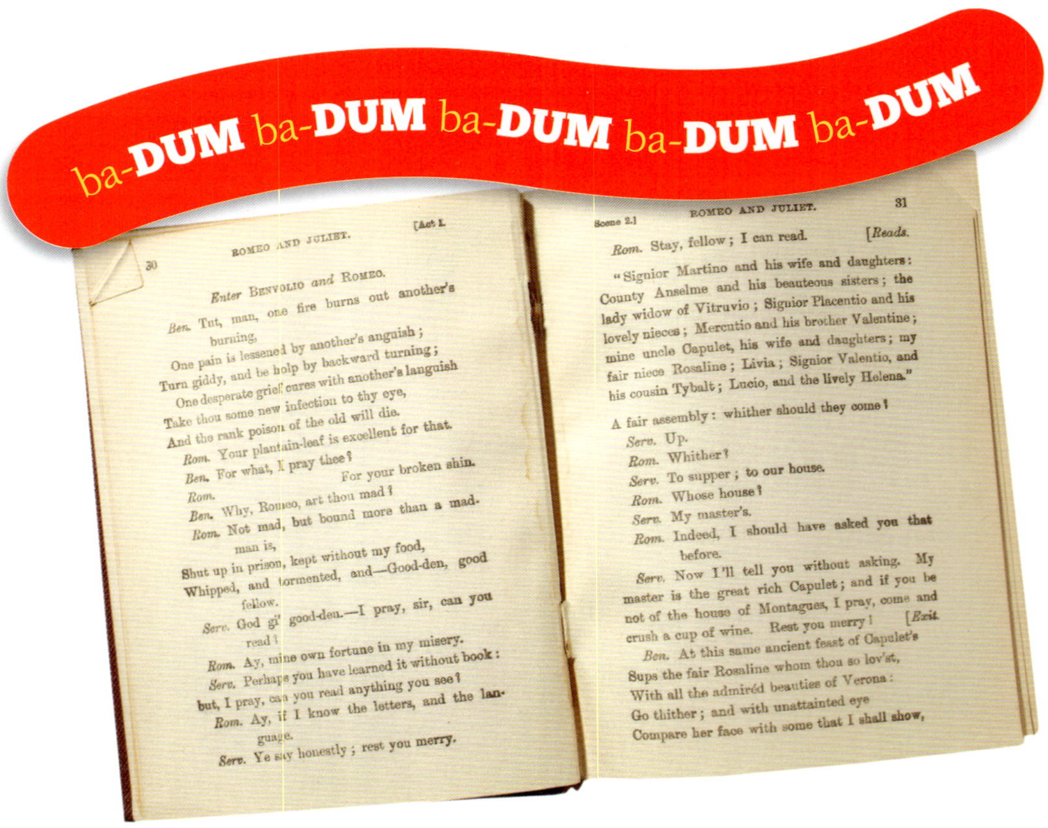

30 ROMEO AND JULIET. [Act I.

Enter BENVOLIO *and* ROMEO.

Ben. Tut, man, one fire burns out another's burning,
One pain is lessened by another's anguish;
Turn giddy, and be holp by backward turning;
One desperate grief cures with another's languish:
Take thou some new infection to thy eye,
And the rank poison of the old will die.
Rom. Your plantain-leaf is excellent for that.
Ben. For what, I pray thee?
Rom. For your broken shin.
Ben. Why, Romeo, art thou mad?
Rom. Not mad, but bound more than a mad-man is,
Shut up in prison, kept without my food,
Whipped, and tormented, and—Good-den, good fellow.
Serv. God gi' good-den.—I pray, sir, can you read?
Rom. Ay, mine own fortune in my misery.
Serv. Perhaps you have learned it without book:
but, I pray, can you read anything you see?
Rom. Ay, if I know the letters, and the language.
Serv. Ye say honestly; rest you merry.

Scene 2.] ROMEO AND JULIET. 31

Rom. Stay, fellow; I can read. [*Reads.*
"Signior Martino and his wife and daughters: County Anselme and his beauteous sisters; the lady widow of Vitruvio; Signior Placentio and his lovely nieces; Mercutio and his brother Valentine; mine uncle Capulet, his wife and daughters; my fair niece Rosaline; Livia; Signior Valentio, and his cousin Tybalt; Lucio, and the lively Helena."
A fair assembly: whither should they come?
Serv. Up.
Rom. Whither?
Serv. To supper; to our house.
Rom. Whose house?
Serv. My master's.
Rom. Indeed, I should have asked you that before.
Serv. Now I'll tell you without asking. My master is the great rich Capulet; and if you be not of the house of Montagues, I pray, come and crush a cup of wine. Rest you merry! [*Exit.*
Ben. At this same ancient feast of Capulet's
Sups the fair Rosaline whom thou so lov'st,
With all the admiréd beauties of Verona:
Go thither; and with unattainted eye
Compare her face with some that I shall show,

Names

The word play related to names in *Romeo and Juliet* is connected to the conflict between the two families, and the rebellion that Romeo and Juliet show as they defy this feud to be together. In Act 2, Scene 1, Juliet speaks of the meaning of names and the fact that their family names are the barrier to her love for Romeo. She realizes that if they renounce their family names, they are merely two people in love. In this simple word play, she chooses to defy her family and their wishes by casting off her name and pledging herself to Romeo.

What's in a name?

"'Tis but thy name that is my enemy,
Thou art thyself though, not a Montague.
What's a Montague? It is nor hand, nor foot,
Nor arm, nor face, nor any other part
Belonging to a man. O, be some other name!
What's in a name? That which we call a rose,
By any other word would smell as sweet;
So Romeo would, were he not Romeo called,
Retain that dear perfection which he owes
Without that title. Romeo, doff thy name,
And for thy name, which is no part of thee,
Take all myself."

Juliet, Act 2, Scene 2

Juliet

Double Meanings

The play is full of double entendres, or words with two meanings. This is best illustrated by Mercutio and the Nurse, who both frequently use puns and words with double meanings, often of a sexual nature. While this provides humor and a bit of a racy edge to the play, it is also in contrast to the kind of love between Romeo and Juliet. While the title characters see their love as almost divine or noble, Mercutio and the Nurse tend to view love in terms of base human desires.

TEACHER NOTES

Video

Of Pentameter & Bear Baiting - Romeo & Juliet Part I: Crash Course English Literature #2

Learn more about the structure and context of *Romeo and Juliet* by watching this video.

1. How does iambic pentameter reflect the natural rhythms of human speech in English while also heightening it? Why does Shakespeare change the meter for the famous line, "O Romeo, Romeo! wherefore art thou Romeo?" Why is Romeo's name the problem?
2. How did Shakespeare navigate between high and low culture? Why is this important?

Weblink

Double Entendre

Explore double entendres by reading this article.

1. Why are there often examples of a pun included in a double entendre?
2. What is the significance of double entendre in literature? Why have they remained popular for so long?

EXTENSION ACTIVITY

Analyzing Bias in a Document

Students will analyze the bias that exists in a document from a different historical time and place, and how that bias shapes the opinions presented in the document. An exemplary analysis of bias in a document will meet the following criteria.

- Identifies the main points presented in the document
- Offers an in-depth interpretation of the document
- Differentiates between facts and opinions
- Identifies the writer
- Presents information about the writer
- Assesses the writer's reliability
- Determines the goals for the document
- Considers and assesses the writer's perspective
- Determines the writer's intended audience
- Identifies when and where the document was written
- Describes the historical context for the time and place in which the document was created, and analyzes how this context might have shaped the opinions expressed in the document
- Infers political or societal influences that may have shaped the opinions presented in the document
- Determines whether the writer had first-hand knowledge of the topic or event, or whether they are reporting as a secondary source
- Determines the document's bias
- Infers what interests the writer might have had that led them to create this document
- Explores other sources related to the topic of the document

Impact of the Play When First Performed

It is believed that *Romeo and Juliet* was written in the mid-1590s, and was likely first performed by 1597. As one of Shakespeare's earlier plays, it was first published in 1597 in his First Quarto, and was included with his other plays in the First Folio in 1623. While not much is known about the earliest production of the play, Shakespeare's tale of star-crossed lovers was on its way to becoming one of his best-known works.

RICHARD BURBAGE

While there are no records describing performances of *Romeo and Juliet* before the Restoration era in Britain, experts believe that Shakespeare's theater company staged the first production of the play after 1660. It is likely that Richard Burbage, who was considered the best actor in London at the time, played the role of Romeo, and a young actor named Robert Goffe may have played the role of Juliet. The play was meant to be performed with a minimalist set, only requiring the stage to have a balcony and trapdoor.

Source Texts

Shakespeare was inspired by a popular story of star-crossed lovers. The story of Romeo and Juliet first came to Elizabethan England in the poem, *The Tragicall Historye of Romeus and Juliet*, written by Arthur Brooke in 1562. The story came from a well-known tale that was published in French and Italian. Brooke translated his poem from a French version. Shakespeare may also have been inspired by Geoffrey Chaucer's *Troilus and Criseyde*, as well as Ovid's *Metamorphoses*, featuring the story of Pyramus and Thisbe.

Female Roles in Shakespeare's Time

When Shakespeare was writing and performing in plays, only men were permitted to act professionally. For this reason, all of the female roles in his plays, including that of Juliet, were performed by young male actors. It was not until 1660, in a revival of *Othello* featuring an actress in the role of Desdemona, that a woman acted in a Shakespearean play.

Other Early Productions

Romeo and Juliet enjoyed many years on the London stage in the seventeenth and eighteenth centuries. In 1679, Thomas Otway adapted the play in a version called *The History and Fall of Caius Marius*, which was set in ancient Rome. This version was the only one performed for about 70 years, until a new version appeared in 1744, staying closer to Shakespeare's original work. One of the most successful versions was that of renowned actor David Garrick, whose production opened at Drury Lane in 1748 and became the standard version used on stage for the next century.

Romeo and Juliet was published in **seven different editions** prior to **1642**.

Romeo and Juliet was likely **first performed** at the **Theatre** and the **Curtain**, two London playhouses used by the Lord Chamberlain's Men.

A **revival** of the play was performed in **1662** in London at **Lincoln's Inn Fields**.

TEACHER NOTES

Document

Shakespeare and gender: the 'woman's part'

Review the article by Claire McManus, published on March 15, 2016, exploring gender in the history of Shakespeare performance.

1. Who do you think is the intended audience for this article? Why? Are the tone and language used appropriate for this audience? Explain your answer.
2. What are the main points of the article and how are they presented? Are these points conveyed effectively to the reader? Why or why not?

Weblink

Richard Burbage

Find out more about Richard Burbage by reviewing this biography.

1. In what ways did Burbage contribute to Shakespeare's popularity? How much of an impact did he have? Why do you think so?
2. The article says that, "[t]he shock and sadness over Burbage's passing may be the key to our understanding of why so little was written on Shakespeare's death just three years earlier." What does this mean? Explain C. C. Stopes's theory in your own words.

EXTENSION ACTIVITY

Writing a Review

Students will write a review of the play. An exemplary review will meet the following criteria.

- Grabs the reader's attention with a creative headline
- Begins with an engaging lead to pull the reader into the article
- Introduces the title of the play, the author, and the genre
- Provides a brief plot description that does not give away the entire story, and makes the reader want to learn more about the play
- Supports arguments about the play with accurate and detailed information
- Organizes the review and its arguments in a concise, clear, and logical manner
- Fits the format and style of a review
- Follows the conventions of print or online journalism
- Demonstrates creativity in their approach
- Writes with a unique, engaging voice and perspective
- Provides fresh insight into the play
- Provides an honest, authentic opinion on the play
- Gives a clear recommendation on the play, backed up by specific textual evidence
- Uses correct spelling, grammar, and punctuation

Impact of the Play Now

More than 400 years after it was written, *Romeo and Juliet* continues to be studied, performed, and enjoyed around the world. Shakespeare's play is one of his best-known stories, and numerous productions are staged every year. This story has been retold in many creative adaptations, and Shakespeare's tale of love and tragedy endures through these retellings.

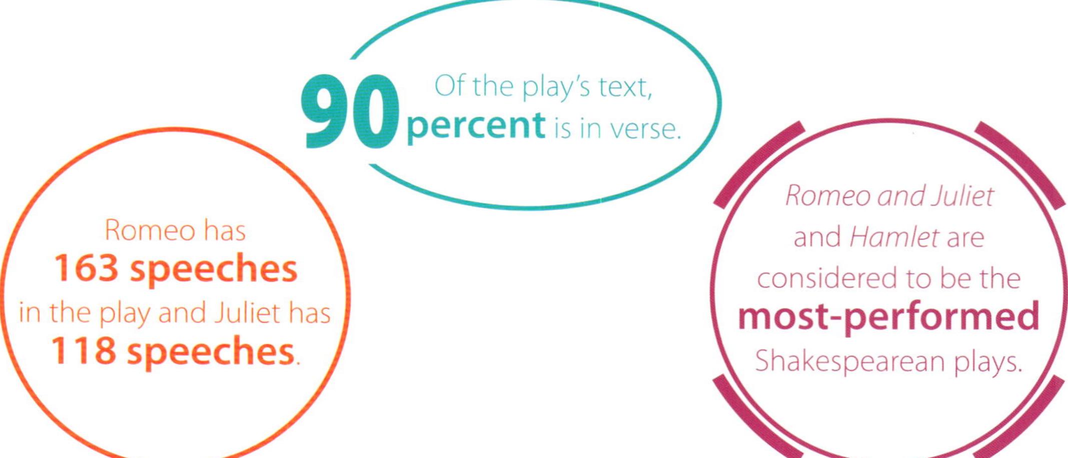

TEACHER NOTES

Document

Romeo and Juliet*, Shakespeare's Globe, London, review: This is an emotionally fierce and fiery *Romeo and Juliet

Examine the review by Paul Taylor, published on May 28, 2017, of Daniel Kramer's production of *Romeo and Juliet*.

1. Do you think that Taylor gives an honest, authentic opinion on the production? Why or why not? Cite evidence from the review to support your position.
2. Who is the intended audience for this play? Based on this review, do you think the play is appropriate for this target audience? Give reasons for your answer. Who would you recommend this performance to and why?

Weblink

***Romeo + Juliet* at 20: Baz Luhrmann's adaptation refuses to age**

Discover more about Baz Luhrmann's adaptation of the play by reading this article, written on the twentieth anniversary of the film's release.

1. The article claims that, "[l]ike its doomed, bullet-bound lovers,… the film refuses to age." Why does the film holds up so well? What reasons does the author give?
2. Watch the trailer for the film embedded in the article. Based on this, how do you think modern audiences might view this adaptation? Explain your answer.

Iconic Adaptation

Some consider *West Side Story* the best adaptation of *Romeo and Juliet*. The 1961 film used the play as the inspiration for a "commentary on race and class in America," which continues to resonate with audiences. In this musical, two gangs, the Caucasian Jets and the Puerto Rican Sharks, battle in New York City, leading to the downfall of the secret romance between Tony, a former Jet, and Maria, the sister of the leader of the Sharks. *West Side Story* has influenced other adaptations of *Romeo and Juliet*, and is often performed as a stage musical.

Creative Retellings

In the 2011 animated film *Gnomeo and Juliet*, two garden gnomes mend the feud between their warring owners, and the story gets an unusually happy ending. The 1998 film *Shakespeare in Love* told a smart, humorous tale of brooding playwright Will Shakespeare and a noblewoman named Viola, who disguises herself to be cast in his play. Gwyneth Paltrow won a Best Actress Oscar for her portrayal of Viola, while Judi Dench won Best Supporting Actress for the role of Elizabeth I. A stage version premiered in Stratford, Ontario, in 2016.

Film Adaptations

One of the most memorable adaptations is the 1996 film directed by Baz Luhrmann, starring Leonardo DiCaprio and Claire Danes. Set in modern-day Verona Beach, California, the Montagues and Capulets become vicious gangs in this flashy film that mixes the original Shakespearean text with an inventive soundtrack. The film received mixed reviews upon release, but is now considered the most influential modern film interpretation of Shakespeare's play.

EXTENSION ACTIVITY

Creating a Timeline

Students will explore a topic related to the play and create a timeline to present their research on historical events connected to this topic. An exemplary timeline will meet the following criteria.

- Includes the most significant events pertaining to the topic to be compared and analyzed
- Includes interesting events
- Uses accurate information for all events, including date, location, and major details
- Orders the events in a chronological sequence
- Describes each event with accurate, vivid, and specific details
- Presents the topic from three or more perspectives
- Inspires the reader to ask thoughtful questions regarding the events and perspectives presented in the timeline
- Uses correct spelling, grammar, and punctuation
- Presents the timeline in a visually attractive and striking manner
- Presents the timeline in a neat, organized manner that is logical and easy to follow
- Uses creativity to present the timeline in an engaging manner
- Effectively communicates the historical information relating to the topic
- Supports each event with reliable sources
- Expresses a clear purpose for creating the timeline
- Enhances the reader's understanding of the topic
- Includes a correctly formatted bibliography of all sources used to create the timeline

Perspectives on Female Shakespearean Roles

Shakespeare created some of the best-known and most challenging roles for women in the history of English theater. In the nineteenth century, to win the role of Juliet was seen as a signifier of a young actress with a promising career ahead of her. Today, playing and winning critical acclaim in difficult, iconic roles such as Ophelia in *Hamlet* and Lady Macbeth in *Macbeth* are still considered to be a mark of an actress's talent.

Timeline of Female Casting in Shakespearean Plays

1600s

1642 Plays are banned in London at the start of the English Civil War, and all of the city's playhouses are closed.

1660 Women are allowed to act professionally in London theaters after the restoration of the English monarchy, due to the aristocracy's interest in professional actresses in France.

1662 Mary Saunderson likely becomes the first woman to play Juliet in a professional theater production.

1664 Writer Samuel Pepys writes that Shakespearean actress Anne Marshall acted "most excellently well as ever I heard woman in my life."

1700s

1782 Sarah Siddons joins the Drury Lane Theater and becomes extremely popular with audiences, and known for her talent on the stage. She is best known for playing Lady Macbeth.

However, it was not until the late seventeenth century that women began tackling Shakespeare's female roles and finding a place for themselves in English theater. The question of gender roles and the ruling ideas of the day dictated perspectives on actresses, who were viewed by society for many years as women of loose morals. Roles that required the female character to dress like a man, such as Portia in *The Merchant of Venice*, Viola in *Twelfth Night*, and Rosalind in *As You Like It*, became popular with male audiences, based on the revealing nature of the actresses' costumes. Today, gender-swapped casting of Shakespearean plays continues to raise questions about the gender politics of theater, as well as create thought-provoking productions of long-beloved plays.

1845 Charlotte Cushman plays the role of Romeo in a London production of *Romeo and Juliet*, with her sister Susan playing the role of Juliet.

1899 French actress Sarah Bernhardt earns critical acclaim across Europe and the United States for her portrayal of Hamlet.

2014 Maxine Peake plays an **androgynous** Hamlet in a production in Manchester, England.

1800s | 1900s | 2000s

1878-1902 Ellen Terry becomes the highest-paid woman in the United Kingdom and the best-known actress of her time, playing a variety of female Shakespearean roles at London's Lyceum Theatre.

1921 Danish actress Asta Nielsen stars in a silent film adaptation of *Hamlet*, in which Hamlet is actually a girl raised as a boy to keep the crown in her family.

2002 A production of *Twelfth Night* at Shakespeare's Globe Theatre features male actors in the roles of Viola and Olivia.

2015 Phyllida Lloyd directs an all-female production of *Henry IV*, running in both London and New York.

TEACHER NOTES

Transparency–Timeline

Timeline of Female Casting in Shakespearean Plays

Examine the historical and cultural contexts shown on the timeline. Then, contrast and correlate its elements with the themes and events presented in *Romeo and Juliet*.

1. In what ways can historical events, culture, and social mores influence a population's perspective on gender equality? How might these elements have shaped the way a reader in the 1590s interpreted the play?
2. How might the era in which William Shakespeare wrote *Romeo and Juliet* have influenced the play's themes and settings? Where in the play is this most evident? Explain your reasoning.
3. Which current events, changes in laws, new ideas, or political discussions are shaping gender equality in the United States today? Which ideas and attitudes are still prevailing? Why?
4. How might current events and present perspectives affect the way a reader interprets the play? Why is it important for readers to understand the era and context in which a play is written?

Writing a Comparative Essay

Students will compare two literary devices used in the play, and then write a comparative essay based on their analysis. An exemplary comparative essay will meet the following criteria.

- Consists of a one-paragraph introduction, three body paragraphs, and a one-paragraph conclusion
- Introduction includes an engaging lead statement about the topic of the essay, more detailed information about the play, and a one-sentence thesis that specifically states the essay's argument
- Body paragraphs include a topic sentence that refers to the thesis and how the idea appears in the play, a supporting sentence that points to this part of the play, textual evidence of this idea from the play, and analysis of this evidence
- Body paragraphs end with a transition to the next paragraph
- Conclusion refers to the topic of the essay and the three points presented in the body paragraphs, and restates the thesis
- Provides a thorough analysis of the literary devices in question
- Cites strong and thorough textual evidence to support analysis of what the play says explicitly
- Presents a clear, specific thesis that indicates a high level of critical engagement
- Organizes ideas in a logical manner
- Communicates arguments in a clear, effective manner
- Properly integrates all quotations
- Correctly cites all sources used
- Correctly formats bibliography

Writing a Comparative Essay

Romeo and Juliet is brought to life with passionate characters, evocative language, and engaging themes that pull the reader into the story. After studying the play, write a comparative essay to explore how two literary devices are used in *Romeo and Juliet*. This could be a comparison of characters, themes, symbols, or settings. To write a comparative essay, you will need to formulate an argument. Your argument should clearly state how you feel your compared elements are similar or different. Support your argument with sufficient evidence from the play and valid reasoning.

How to Analyze and Compare Characters

Use the chart to guide your comparison of two characters in *Romeo and Juliet*.

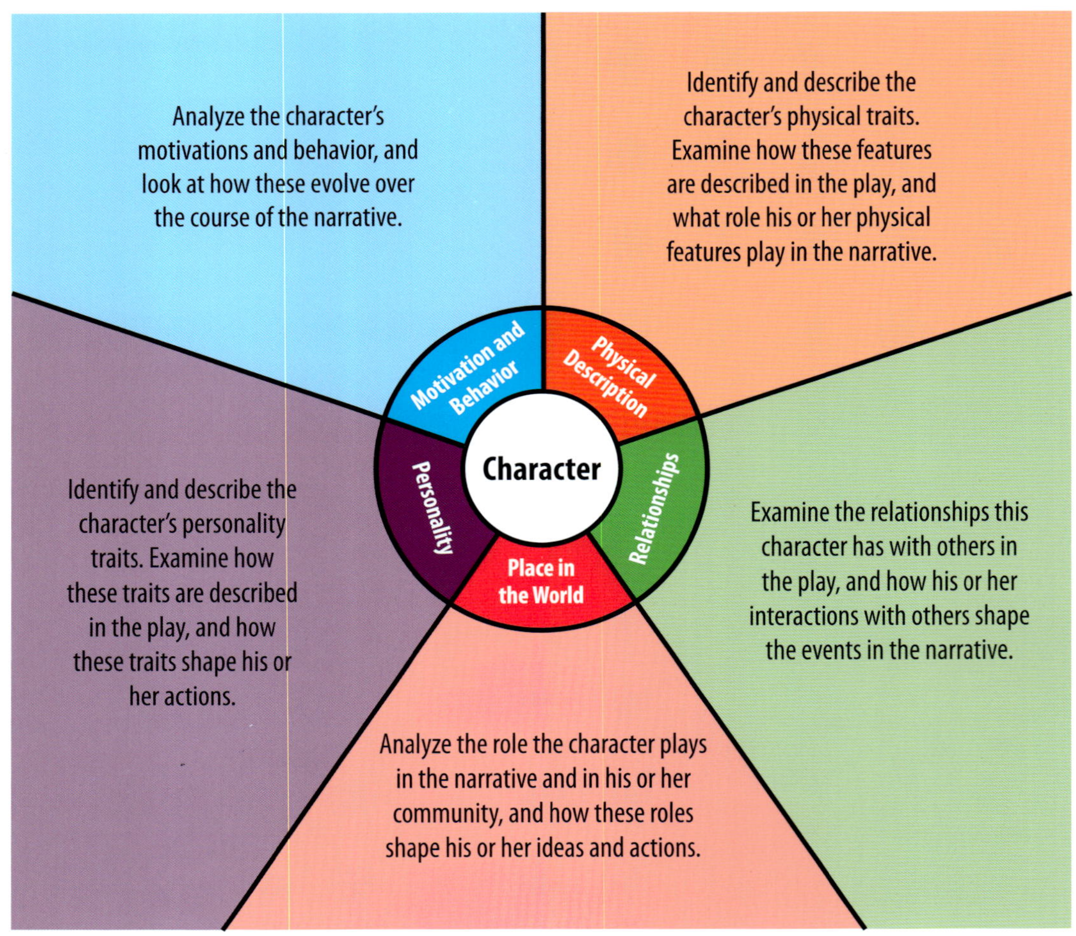

Comparing Romeo and Mercutio

Personality
- Intense and passionate in all his emotions
- Smart
- Sensitive
- Idealistic
- Loyal

Place in the World
- From a prominent family in Verona
- Not interested in taking part in the fighting between his family and the Capulets

Motivation and Behavior
- Devoted to his friends
- Willing to face numerous obstacles to be with Juliet
- Matures throughout the play
- Understanding of love evolves
- More interested in love than violence
- Would rather die than live without Juliet
- Hopes his relationship could help end the feud
- Does not want to fight Tybalt, but finds he must take revenge

Relationships
- Son of Montague and Lady Montague
- Mercutio's best friend
- Cousin of Benvolio
- Brooding over Rosaline at the beginning of the play
- Falls in love with Juliet

Physical Description
- About 16 years old
- Described by Juliet as handsome

Place in the World
- Spends his time with the Montague family
- Dislikes the Capulets

Motivation and Behavior
- Has a strong sense of honor
- Disguises his world-weariness and skepticism with wit and sexual innuendo
- Mocks those with romantic ideals
- Believes love is nothing more than sexual desire
- Dislikes affected and pretentious people
- Motivated by honor and loyalty to his friends

Physical Description
- Young
- Not physically described

Relationships
- Romeo's best friend
- Friends with Benvolio
- Related to Prince Escalus
- Unaware of Romeo's relationship with Juliet
- Hates Tybalt

Personality
- Wild
- Playful
- Brooding
- Cynical
- Sarcastic and witty
- Hot-headed
- Imaginative

TEACHER NOTES

Transparency–Chart

Questions for Character Analysis
Analyze how specific character features, such as conflicts, motivations, relationships, place in the world, and personality affect the plot of *Romeo and Juliet*. Cite strong and thorough textual evidence to support your analysis of what the play says explicitly as well as the inferences you may have drawn from the play's setting, themes, and symbols.

Quiz Answers

1. B
2. C
3. B
4. A
5. A
6. B
7. D
8. A
9. B
10. C

Key Words

androgynous: of indeterminate gender

fate: the inevitable outcome of something, thought to be predestined and out of a person's control

feud: a continuous state of conflict between two parties

gender roles: standards for behavior relating to a person's gender, as considered acceptable by society

inhibitions: feelings of restraint that prevent one from acting on his or her natural instincts

interpretation: a specific, personal way of explaining what something represents

loyalty: a strong feeling of support toward a person, place, or idea

morals: principles of what is right and wrong

perspectives: certain points of view or positions regarding a subject

Renaissance: a movement or period of vigorous artistic and intellectual activity

society: an organized community of people interacting with each other

universal: present everywhere; widely accepted

Literary Terms

antagonist: the character who stands in opposition to the protagonist; in some cases, the antagonist creates or represents the conflict that the protagonist faces

climax: the moment of greatest tension in the story's action

conflict: a struggle between two or more opposing forces, creating a tension that must be resolved

exposition: the beginning of the story, where the characters and setting are introduced

falling action: the events that take place after the climax, leading up to the end of the story

Freytag's Pyramid: a narrative structure consisting of five elements, including exposition, rising action, climax, falling action, and resolution

genre: a specific category of an artistic work based on topic, form, or style

metaphor: a comparison between two things made by stating a connection without using "like" or "as"

mood: the overall feeling that the narrative is intended to evoke within the reader

narrative: a logically arranged series of events presented for an audience; a story

oxymoron: a combination of two words that have opposing meanings

personification: the attribution of human traits to something that is not human to give it a more vibrant description

plot: the specific action that propels a story forward

poetry: language that is spoken or written according to some pattern that is generally rhythmic

prose: the ordinary form of spoken or written language, most often used in stories

protagonist: the central character in a piece of fiction who must deal with a conflict and often undergoes some type of change as a result

resolution: the end of the story, when the problems are resolved and the action comes to a conclusion

rising action: the events that create increased drama or tension

symbolism: a stylistic device using symbols to represent and intensify concepts and ideas

theme: the underlying idea or position in a work that is often a general, universal statement about life

Index

LIGHTBOX

SUPPLEMENTARY RESOURCES

Click on the plus icon found in the bottom left corner of each spread to open additional teacher resources.

- Download and print the book's quizzes and activities
- Access curriculum correlations
- Explore additional web applications that enhance the Lightbox experience

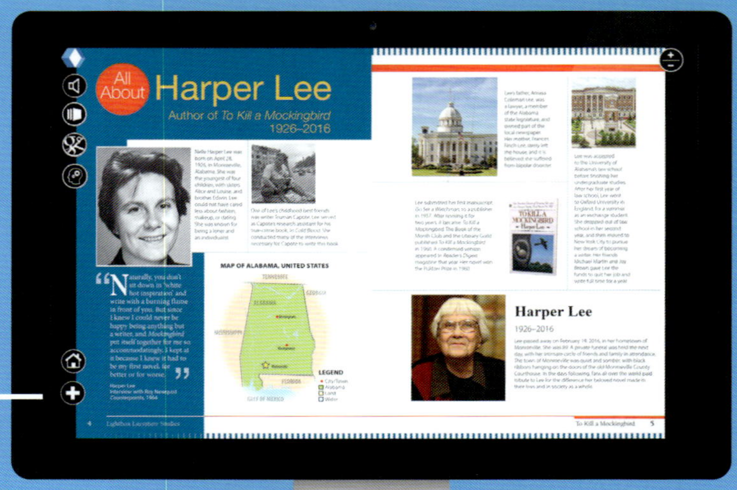

LIGHTBOX DIGITAL TITLES

Packed full of integrated media

VIDEOS

INTERACTIVE MAPS

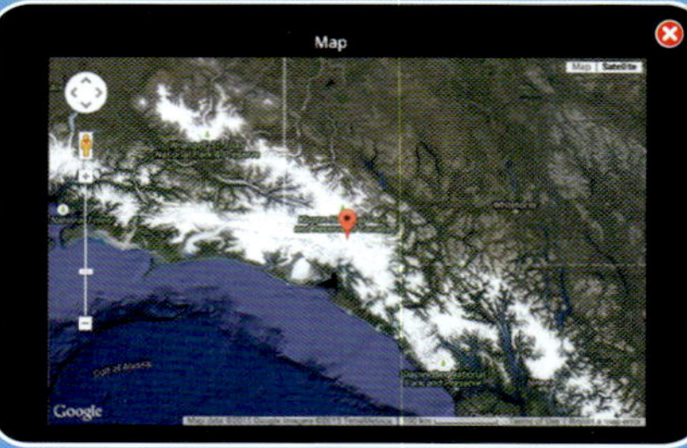

WEBLINKS

SLIDESHOWS

QUIZZES

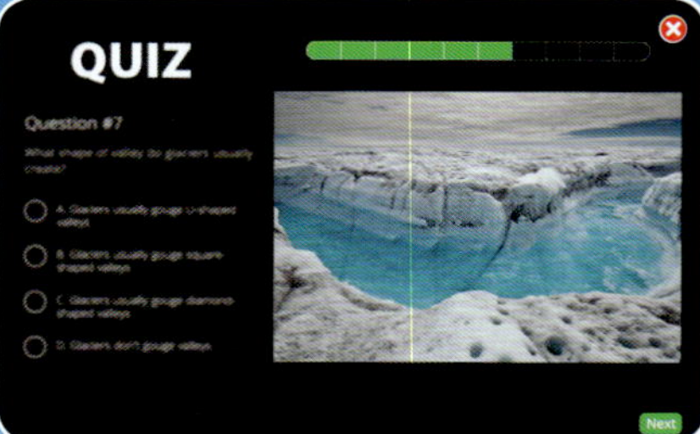

OPTIMIZED FOR

- ✓ TABLETS
- ✓ WHITEBOARDS
- ✓ COMPUTERS
- ✓ AND MUCH MORE!

Published by Smartbook Media Inc.
276 5th Avenue, Suite 704 #917
New York, NY 10001
Website: www.openlightbox.com

Copyright © 2018 Smartbook Media Inc.
All rights reserved. No part of this publication may be reproduced, stored in a retrieval system, or transmitted in any form or by any means, electronic, mechanical, photocopying, recording, or otherwise, without the prior written permission of the publisher.

Library of Congress Cataloging-in-Publication Data

Names: Whelan, Piper, author.
Title: Romeo and Juliet / Piper Whelan.
Description: New York, NY : Smartbook Media Inc., [2018] | Series: Lightbox literature studies | Includes index.

Identifiers: LCCN 2016056381 (print) | LCCN 2017015552 (ebook) | ISBN 9781510520080 (multi-user ebk.) | ISBN 9781510520073 (hard cover : alk. paper)
Subjects: LCSH: Shakespeare, William, 1564-1616. Romeo and Juliet--Examinations--Study guides. | Tragedy--Examinations--Study guides.
Classification: LCC PR2831 (ebook) | LCC PR2831 .W54 2018 (print) | DDC 822.3/3--dc23
LC record available at https://lccn.loc.gov/2016056381

Printed in Guangzhou, China
2 3 4 5 6 7 8 9 0 26 25 24 23 22

062022
220610

Editor: Katie Gillespie
Art Director: Terry Paulhus

Every reasonable effort has been made to trace ownership and to obtain permission to reprint copyright material. The publisher would be pleased to have any errors or omissions brought to its attention so that they may be corrected in subsequent printings.

The publisher acknowledges Getty Images, iStock, Alamy, and Shutterstock as its primary image suppliers for this title